THE DARK IS WHEN I LOVE

DR. PRATIK BHAT
(THE DARK POET)

Presentation by *BookLeaf Publishing*

Web: www.bookleafpub.com

E-mail: info@bookleafpub.com

ISBN : 9789363314924

First edition 2024

For Saumya

ACKNOWLEDGEMENT

I extend my gratitude to my wife, mom, dad, and brother for their unwavering belief and support. Thank you for always being there.

I'm indebted to the readers of my books for their faith and encouragement. Your enthusiasm inspires me to keep writing.

A shout-out to my publisher for making the publishing process smooth as margarine.

And heartfelt thanks to my editor, Ivy Thomas, for their meticulous work and insightful feedback, which greatly enhanced the book.

OBSIDIAN

You bleed into me,
Your poison unholy.
I see you standing there,
With an arm twisted,
From an accident.
You scream,
As if fatality is nothing.
In the night I see a vision,
That you will endure.
I give you my life,
One life that remains with me.
For I have loved you endlessly.
Beyond the dark mountains and the dark pond,
I see you lay now,
Recklessly,
With another woman,
Who doesn't even want you.
Patiently she draws out a sword,
Swiftly makes a cut,
A hole in your heart exists now,
And it bleeds mercilessly.
But I had only one life to give you.
You got killed,
By another.
Now I wait for you to come,

Beside me,
As I slowly watch you bleed,
Endlessly.

BLACK GROUND COFFEE

I watch you sip,
Your coffee,
Black.
No sugar,
Forget the whipped cream;
How can you taste it so acrimonious?
How could you be bitter to me?
Sweet divine sensations as you,
Kill me and strip me naked,
Only to uncouth me.
In my youth you betrayed me;
You took my virginity and I don't know
Why I gave it to you.
You then laughed as we came together,
With that grin on your face.
I knew you would leave me to my remains.
Now my head is just above sand,
I'm sinking in deep,
With no way out.
You don't even need me anymore.
You just watch me,
As I
Rot.

YOU DISGUST ME

You wounded me,
By saying unreal things to me.
I was yours,
And you were mine—
So I contemplated.
Now you tear me apart.
My consistency now,
Molten cheesecake from a microwave.
You disgust me with,
All the things you do,
All the things you did.
I rise above you,
Only to find you spread,
Black moss,
All over me,
With slits and maps of fungus,
Propagating and devouring me.
I raise my hand to escape;
But it grasps me,
In its entirety.
I grow cold,
As I see a blood moon,
Above me.
I end myself,
As I slit my wrists and see,

My red flow,
A new pool of blood,
Encircles me.
I am a blood moon on the ground,
Where not a soul can
Save me!

THE RITUAL ON THE BEACH

I see a skull,
Lying there,
On the beach,
At a far-flung corner,
Where no one can
Reach.
And another limb,
Dissected and soggy,
Away from the skull.
It was not an untainted bone,
But with flesh intact.
I see a crab,
About it.
Monster walking in
Circles, like a ritual.
An eagle elegantly comes down,
Piercing through the atmosphere,
Reaching for the leg,
To feast on the flesh.
It would pluck out chunks,
And devour you fast.
I stop it from doing so.
I find a necklet around the flesh;
It holds an initial,

I remember the name,
I have seen this afore,
It was me who gifted it to you.
In my childhood,
You were my crush,
Until your dad got a transfer,
To a faraway kingdom.
How the fuck
Are you here!
Like some ritual performed,
On the beach,
Dead with only bits and pieces of you,
Lingering.
I call the police,
They come after what seems to be a day.
I read a news article the next day,
Remnants of a girl found astray,
Serial killer at large.
The name displayed,
Was of another man,
Whom you dated.
He was a serial killer.
He was our classmate who killed
A rabbit,
And feasted on it,
Was sent to juvenile court.
Of course we were small.
Now see what has become of you!
Why did you date,

A murderer,
And why not me?
I would have kept you blooming,
And safe,
With me.

HAPPY FUCKING BIRTHDAY!

Your birthday was today,
Not yesterday,
Not tomorrow.
A party underway,
I was invited,
But I didn't want to come,
I didn't want to go.
I wanted to see you cry,
I wanted to be the one,
Who would never wish you,
On your birthday.
To the stars and the moon,
You shone in the
Starlight.
A wreath of roses,
On top of your cranium.
Candies and jalebis,
No kaju barfi,
No nicotine.
I go out,
To catch a smoke.
Your call keeps coming,
I know my fucking ringtone,
I silence my phone.

I know you are,
My so-called girlfriend,
But you hang out with all and sundry,
Like a toy you treated me.
I am so desolate and lost,
I have to ruin your birthday.
If not,
Ruin me.
I go back to where you are,
I see you from close not far.
You are busy with another man,
Endlessly ruining my mind again.
I don't trust you at all,
You slept with that guy,
That DJ from the club,
Because you liked his tunes.
I was sober and average,
I was in my mind,
Never lost,
Craved to be found,
By you.
As you see me,
Noticing you,
Talking to another,
You leave that bloke,
Canter to me.
I turn my back,
And walk away.
Go and die!

It's not my fucking birthday
Anyways!

YOU CAN'T BE SERIOUS!

I see you palpate me,
With your eyes a heavy red,
You were in anger.
A handsome livid untried man,
Cute in an orange hoodie.
You were sunsetting,
Into my soul,
In an endless combat of my mind and
Not acquiring you.
I was haemorrhaging;
My hearts crevice,
A never-ending river,
Of crimson.
I showered myself,
To clean off whatever sins,
I must have done,
In my past life.
And you were a Seraph,
You got the best,
Always.
I passed you through that corridor,
You didn't even dare,
To look at me,
While I saw those beads of sweat,
On your forehead,

As you were anxious.
Were you getting a panic attack?
I know you would,
After what I have done,
To you.
I wrote a love letter,
To our lady principal,
Addressing how her assets were
As big as the moon,
Signed off with your name.
I am a calligrapher,
I can copy handwriting.
There is no way anyone can identify,
That it's not yours.
I hear the true rumours,
As it reaches my inner hair cells.
You have been expelled from school.
The star student,
Gone forever.
I always came second,
In class,
You first.
Now there is no chance,
Of me ever coming second again.
I adored you,
I wanted you,
I proposed you,
You didn't even give me closure.
You had everything on your side,

My side wasn't worth it,
In an endless divine mess,
I prayed diurnally to the darkness,
To arrest you from haunting me.
My Soul will now,
Finally be,
In concord!

OUR KINGDOM BLOWN AWAY

Through kingdoms we trod,
Angels and demons,
All in our way.
We still fought them and succeeded,
Cause we battled them together.
Together is when,
We could overcome it all,
Make kingdoms tumble,
Make the seven seas roar.
On a ship we lay,
So careless so dismayed,
As the clear skies grew darker,
A lightning strikes,
Not at the boat,
But you.
You are now a barbecued hen,
You fall down,
And get misplaced.
As your ash is blown away,
By the wind,
I try to gather you,
But I can't gather enough,
Of you.
I can't even cry.

I just try to process what just happened,
I am hypnotised as I see,
A bright light,
Through the clouds;
It looked deific,
It looked chaotic,
I feel myself levitate,
I feel myself glow,
I then understood I wore metal,
And thunder struck me too.

THE STAIN

We went for fine dining,
You wore a stainless white shirt,
I wore polka-dot pyjamas.
I didn't care if it was,
Fine dining or dining,
At a roadside kiosk.
I was sleeping peacefully,
Till you emerged in front of my home,
Asking me to leave my comforts,
You called me out and took me for a drive.
We go to that 5-star,
By the Palace Lake,
Greeted with a shehnai,
And apple pie.
I drowned in its zest,
My mouth now dripping wet,
I lost my touch with reality,
Till you forced me to sit down.
Then you get me wine,
I ask you what's the occasion?
Why did you drag me down here?
I was in my deepest stagnation,
You disturbed me,
You said that as your paramour,
You expected me to be faithful.

I took the wine bottle from the waiter,
Smashed it on you,
As the glass shards spear you,
In multiple areas of your skin,
I see the stainless white shirt turn red,
As red wine never forgets to leave a stain.
Everyone gets alarmed around us,
They look at me,
I am in calm composure.
I know I had an affair,
With your best friend,
And ditched him for you.
You found out,
But who cares,
What's done is done.
No one questions me like this.
As the paramedics come with law enforcement,
I say you were trying to drug me to sleep.
Wasn't it obvious to them,
That I was in my pyjamas,
I did look sleepy,
I said in self defence,
I smashed your head,
Into smithereens.
I know I will be left scot-free,
I know nothing will happen,
I'll make an Instagram page now,
As all reporters surround me,
I'll already be famous by tomorrow,

I'll gain millions of followers in a day.
I am exultant and amused,
Things go as planned,
After all.
I smile,
Looking at myself through the mirror,
My reflection haunts me as I see,
Another personality hidden within!

YOU BETRAY ME

It was exam time,
I felt you next to me,
We shared adjacent tables,
I wanted you to aid me,
I would fail if you would not,
Cause all I did was stare at you in class,
And not study.
Only study you.
How your hair flowed like
A waterfall crashing!
Your eyes were of the perfect size,
Your iris looked Irish,
Though you were Indian,
And I was always stunned.
I 'shoo' you to signal you,
I knew we never talked;
But what is this happening?
You don't look at me at all,
Maybe you were sincere,
I give you the benefit of the doubt,
But then I see you,
Twist and turn,
Your nose like a beak,
Pointing to him—
The class genius,

Who flirted with you.
You were the most picturesque,
In class,
I was run-of-the-mill, at best.
You give him a flying kiss,
When the invigilator looks away,
And then he gives you a page,
Full of answers, and me—
I am left to decay.
As I 'shoo' at you again,
You look at me with a blank stare,
And then you get up and grumble about me,
To the invigilator for harassment.
I am disqualified from the exam,
I am sent to the principal's cabin,
My parents are called,
To assist me and arrest me.
I am going to lose another year.
Yes, I'm the failure of the class,
And fuck, I'll be here again,
In the same class,
Same bench.
But you won't be here,
To
Stare.

THE PARTY

Oh! Fucking hell,
Today we are going to the party.
Break the rules,
Break hearts,
Ask our bills,
To be paid by the men,
At the bar,
Who want us in bed,
Stripped naked for them.
But I would never do,
Anything as such.
I just go,
To save money,
Flirt,
To save money.
I love it when men,
Spend on me,
Insane currency,
That I get experience,
Which otherwise,
I could never get.
But,
The party must go on,
Without anything to stop us.
I did kill a man once,

Inside a barn he took me,
Imposed himself on me,
In my childhood.
I took a pike,
Which lay there,
Stabbed the man,
Into his chest,
As blood spilled,
His lungs deflated,
All over me.
I could never make love,
Again,
Even to myself.
But hell yeah!
Fucking hell yeah!
What's done is done,
The party is underway,
The DJ plays the creamiest descant,
While I am armed with a gun now,
To save myself,
Till the music,
Washes itself,
Away.

DON'T COME BACK

You come to me,
After a week,
Devoting your time,
To that mademoiselle.
You don't know,
What has,
Gone through,
My head.
Traversed dimensions did I,
Universes that unfold mysteries I seek,
I found at that bottomless pit,
A snake with a fang so sharp and sleek,
I took the snake and preserved it with caution,
As you come home saying,
The conference at Shimla went awesome.
I take you to sleep,
Strip down your clothes,
You are limp, though
You have over-utilised your
Privates.
I cast a spell,
You have no clue,
What's about to happen,
As I blindfold you,
And then take out the snake,

Carefully I have been trained,
By the best snake charmer,
From the southern district.
As I make it bite,
Your floppy asset,
I watch you scream,
As your 'limp-on' becomes,
A hard-on swelling,
As blood drips down,
I leave you there,
Lock the room,
I go for a trip,
To the Himalayas now,
To wash away,
My necessary sins.

BEDLAM

Romance is nothing but
A far away princess,
For whom,
Tiny soldiers and,
Princes without pride,
Seek for,
In the abyss of the plentiful,
Where the mouth of a river opens up into,
A devastating whirlpool,
Where the screams of the ancient,
And the decidual uterus
Of new life,
Shines.
We hunt for something,
That doesn't exist,
Giving up oneself,
Into an eternal flame,
That never loses its fire because,
A fool like you will always be there,
To dive into,
The never-ending,
Pandemonium.

WORLD-WEARY

In that temple by the lake,
We entered,
Unceremoniously.
We were plain as daylight,
I know you prayed for me,
For my well-being,
For our relationship,
That should prosper,
And you cared for me.
I had a heart attack,
Where I almost died,
Though young.
You wanted me,
To have faith in God.
I did pray,
That day,
Beside you,
To be,
Not beside you.
I did pray,
To God,
To end us,
I am jaded,
It's a crying shame that,
We cling on to each other,

Even though we both know,
We should separate.
We were never the right fit,
Opposites may attract;
But I choose to distract myself
From you,
Only to cause myself,
More harm,
Than good.
I know things were,
Always harsh for you.
But why do we persist,
When we could be happier,
Without each other?
I watch you as you bleed,
But you choose to stay with me,
Knowing you will not get anyone,
Better than me.
But I have long been away,
Into another's arm.
A twisted tale,
Of self-love and,
Self-exploitation,
Letting myself get used,
By several,
That remain—
Now ghouls are those souls.
I have ghosted them,
For far too long,

Just for you,
Just for us,
To be together,
Which we will,
Never be,
Though physically,
Close.

COSMIC LOVERS

Out of this world,
Out of our sordid minds,
We took a pill,
Then we had a kiss.
As I was being pulled away from you,
The pill made the world slow down.
We entered another dimension,
That was so crystal clear,
Everything that was real,
Seemed unreal that day,
Surreal, things were.
At a point I lost myself,
I thought I was you,
Staring at myself,
My stark-naked soul,
With my heart outside my chest,
I could see it beat,
In unrest.
I could see us float,
As if we were dead.
All I thought about was,
How do we go back,
As we entered another dimension,
Within this dimension,
That was already not tangible.

I could hear the voices,
Of the Ancient People,
Already dead;
So were
We.

WILL YOU MARRY ME?

Strawberry beer,
A New York cheesecake,
A walnut brownie,
With chunks of nuts,
And soda bubbles
That pop,
The right way into your
Mouth.
As I look at you,
Inhaling everything,
Of what I say,
I only wonder;
How we could be together,
Without tying the knot?
Society is okay,
Marriage is an invention.
Are we supposed to marry?
Are we supposed to bring children
To this world to toil?
Or is it a lunar eclipse,
Hiding the light from,
The eyes of the innocent?
But as I see you,
Cough out,
The last of your strawberry beer,

All over me,
I exhale myself,
From you,
And tell you—
It's time to depart,
I have used you abundantly,
Let me move on,
To another soul,
Until I find the right one.
Does the right one even exist,
Or are we all one
Fucking ourselves
Over and over
Again?

FULFIL MY DESIRES

You got a new cycle.
You cycled yourself,
Directly to my doorstep.
It was incredible,
How you were a fledgling;
I was older than you,
I didn't like mature men,
I loved the immature,
Whom I could sculpt,
To perfection.
So was my plan,
To sculpt you.
We were far away,
Faded from the light.
You had a girlfriend,
In a remote town.
But you were rich and now,
Within my reach.
I wanted to make myself better,
Not your existence more comfortable.
I wanted to make you distant and away,
From your actual girlfriend.
As you park your cycle,
And show it to me,
I ask you to come in.

I get wet just staring at you,
Chiselled jaw and,
A heaving chest,
As if you wore,
Armour beneath.
I ask you for tea,
But you are already here,
Next to me.
You push me on my settee,
You melt into me,
Like plastic on fire.
I guide you through,
Looks like you are,
A virgin non-virgin,
Who doesn't know how to make moves.
You must be out of your mind,
As you try different moves,
That run me dry.
I push you away,
I say we can be,
Just friends,
And just that,
Maybe I do need,
A mature man,
To fulfil my desires.
You are too unripe,
Too juvenile,
That I am sure,
You will never be able to,

Fulfil your
Own desires.

MANGOES AND CURVES

Floating on a pool,
Over an inflatable round doughnut
Of a seat,
I stroke,
To reach your feet.
You are at the corner,
Of the pool,
On the artificial rocky edge,
Stark naked.
You don't even wear,
A leaf,
That falls from the Mango tree,
Inclined towards the pool;
It's old now.
As I ask you to plunge in,
I meant dive into me.
You resist at first,
But after a few splashes,
You dart to a corner,
And dive into me.
I hold you from behind,
I cup your chest,
Those curves are unholy,
My hands are
In pure unrest,
As I move through,

Feel them through and through,
I want them,
To be in my memory,
Forever,
Even when I'm not with you.
But then the old ancient mango tree,
Falls.
It was many years old,
I had warned you to banish it,
But your love for flora,
Made us separated,
From realism,
That it could damn fall,
On us!
As I shriek,
You keep staring,
As a branch which was pointy,
Pierces through your
Left breast,
Piercing first through my left hand,
That was holding it.
I am in the hospital now,
My hand amputated.
You are in the cemetery,
Waiting for me.
The only memory of you with me,
Is your curve,
That I never felt,
Before.

THE LAST KISS

I contrived you,
But you never knew I did.
You were in a mood of decay,
While I imagined you,
Built you from scratch.
You try to run away from me,
You say you are too unadulterated,
To be with someone like me,
Who is imperfect.
I didn't know it came to this!
I clearly want to shut you down,
But your soul is under my control.
You are my soul and a part of me.
I ask you for your hand,
Which you first resist.
I touch your hand,
And guide it away,
From you,
As I lay a kiss.
I place your hand,
On your own neck
And give you a directive,
Where you squeeze your hand,
Knowing,
You would squeeze yourself,

Out of life.
But what is this?
You don't follow my order,
You fucking artificial robot!
When did you
Change the codes,
Given by me?
The lenses of your eyes,
Become laser beams,
As they pass through,
The centre of my
Forehead.
I can only see you now,
Embedding your last kiss,
Onto me.

THE CELIBATE

You never wedded,
You are passing on your life,
Like nothing matters.
Not even you!
You bring women,
Into that mansion of yours,
Laid deep,
In that deep jungle,
Where you pace,
To reach your paradise,
Women in and out,
You tread deep within them,
In and out,
But not one can put off your eternal fire.
You never get,
What you want.
I always wanted you.
I used to go,
Higher and higher,
Looking at you.
We had decided on marriage,
Everything was fixed,
You broke it in a wink,
Saying your age,
Wasn't the right fit.

Now you wait,
As you age,
Like a lion with a grey mane,
As you go boundlessly,
With the amount of souls,
You devour,
I watch you,
Destroy yourself,
As I have always destroyed you,
By not influencing you to marry me,
By letting you go,
To see you happy,
I see you rot,
Like a rat expired,
You stink.
I will watch you,
As you die,
A celibate.

UNCONDITIONAL

Growing psychotic,
I see you,
You first had to finish off,
Your pills,
Crushed into your lunch,
Coz, you don't consume them,
On time.
You are a bitch,
You see,
For not listening to me,
For ruining yourself,
For deteriorating yourself to shambles,
For trying an assortment of drugs,
Chronically.
I got a call,
From a friend,
That you were admitted,
You have started hallucinating,
You hear the voices of the primordial,
Commanding you,
To exterminate yourself.
You envision things out of this realm,
You cannot distinguish,
What's real from fake.
In multiple realities you subsist,

You have shat your pants in the pursuit,
Of counterfeit happiness.
Now I, your father, have to clean you up.
Your mother is dead,
She was a schizophrenic too.
Genetic transmission I see,
But I told you not to do drugs.
You have exacerbated an illness,
That will consume you,
Entirely.
From childhood you imagined a twin,
Who I always supported to exist.
Now I divulge that,
I saw nonentity,
You only remind me,
Of your dead mother now,
And I suffer,
Even though I'm normal,
I suffer,
My life bound,
To you,
In unconditional love.

DUMPED AT MY GRANDMOTHER'S MANSION

I was a lad,
At my grandmother's mansion,
Eating Besan Ladoo and
Whipped cream on my apple pie.
I get bored,
Of going there,
My parents had left,
For an excursion,
I wasn't invited.
I was just here,
Getting stuffed,
With swollen up cheeks,
With a swollen-up belly,
A stout child,
Was I.
As the night came by,
I exited the villa,
The silence felt like sin.
It was chilly and I just wore shorts.
I went to the adjacent woodland,
Where all I could see,
Was pure darkness.

Not even a ray,
Of light,
From the moon,
Could penetrate.
I walk slowly,
I could hear twigs break,
The creaking only worsened,
The more fastidious I was,
I saw creepy-crawlies that glowed,
I heard roars of beasts unknown,
I heard murmurs of people talking,
Though no one else was there around,
No matter how many times,
I gazed around,
Hurting my neck.
I then reach an area,
Where the trees failed to cover.
The moonbeam passed through the fissure,
I could finally make my mind recover,
As I see the spotlight,
In the middle of the deep dark timberland,
It felt calm suddenly,
A pond the moonbeam lit,
I go to the edge,
I feel like going in for a swim,
Then I see a face—
The frontage of you!
My crush from summer school.
I blush and blush,

As I feel tentacles on my feet,
I'm wrenched into the pond,
I yelp into the silence,
It echoes back to me.
My vision fades like a veil,
In front of me.
Suddenly I am woken up,
By my grandmother's yell
"Get up lad, it's time for
Some poha and
Tea!"
I try to get up,
But I am paralysed,
From my foot to head.
The only contraption I can see,
Is the
Ceiling fan,
Now falling on,
Me.

OPPOSITE OF BASIC

The foliage

Glints,

I see the leaves move,

Unhurried,

With the breeze.

I see sunlight and moonlight,

Shine on them,

In synchrony.

I see flowers,

Their colour, too vibrant.

Now,

I see wires,

From the DJ set,

Look like,

Snakes that have,

Come alive,

Slowly slithering.

I see a table-top fan,

Placed,

In front of a sleeping beauty.

The weather is fiery now,

So is her majesty,

As I can make out,

Every strand of her hair,

Shuffle.

I see that she is more animate,
Than a fish out on the shore.
I see the clock,
It ticks gradually now.
I see my wrist,
I see wrinkles formed.
I see skyscrapers,
From afar.
I see paint,
Trickle out from the concrete
Walls.
I look at a diamond,
It twinkles now,
Like a kaleidoscope of beams,
Of different intensities,
Falling onto my eyeballs.
I take a breath now,
I try to walk,
The ground feels,
So cushiony,
I can't feel it anymore,
I feel like I'm floating away—
No gravity.
I then transcend beyond time and space,
Only to see,
A real cherub—
Not what I had in mind.
Nonetheless,
I see it has,

Infinite corners,
Infinite sentiments,
Infinite insignias,
With only one mutable eye,
Looking into me.
I look into it,
And it gives me,
A blindness,
That I can't perceive or explain.
And the next thing I know,
Is another ethereal force,
Asking me to write,
Asking my hands to,
Bleed.

THE DARK POET

Take me away,
Into the seven seas.
Take me away,
Show me a habitation,
So unhallowed,
That my soul could liquesce,
And turn black,
But, that would be the norm,
That would be acceptable,
For all souls lingering,
In that area,
Are dark.
And, the murky is where,
I surrender.
The opaque is where,
I find love
And
Peace.

LOVE AT FIRST SIGHT

I glimpsed at everything
On parade—
Cheesecakes,
Hazelnut doughnuts
Glazed,
Unglazed dough-balls,
Red velvet,
Black Forest
Cakes.
Oh!
Then I see you.
You look like a dessert,
In red.
Like a cherry, your nose
Gets flushed,
As you see me staring at you,
Like a dog for a bone,
Saliva dripping from the edges
Of my lips,
Now wet,
To feel yours;
I have never seen anyone so impeccable.
I only want to take a bite,
Out of you,
Until I hear,

A chime from the door.
A man, looking average
Enters,
Staring at me,
Staring at you,
Then goes to your side,
And waits,
As you greet him.
Your boyfriend!
I figure it out.
I take my time,
But I figure it out.
But what can I do?
Was I at fault?
You looked like a marshmallow,
That could melt in my mouth.
I'm allured,
I crave to try you,
Or maybe,
Let no one try you.
This man I have seen
On the news,
A news reporter he was,
Of a channel that,
No one watches.
Are you his wife?
I see you have no ring.
But he does!
I go to his profile,

He is married already.
Do you even know this?
I strive to know,
I want to melt into you,
Without you in my life,
I am unfaithful,
To my existence.
I go up to you,
I say I need you.
You use pepper spray,
I get blinded,
I flinch,
I squirm on the ground.
Your so-called already married boyfriend,
Kicks me in my balls.
I can feel the ache soar high,
My one eye unblinded—
Only one eye sprayed.
Like a Cyclops I get up,
I see a baker's knife for cake,
A long one indeed,
It seemed sharp,
I clasp it in my hand,
As he runs towards me,
I swing at him;
The force,
Decapitates him.
This knife is no baker's knife!
It was sharp like a butcher's knife.

I see his head swing into the air,
Then tumble
On the ground,
Then halt
In a pool of bloody liquid,
Where his body lay,
Already decompressed,
And plummeted,
His head
Turned to me,
His eyeballs
Stuck on me,
In a horrendous stare.
I know I can't have you now,
Neither can he.
It doesn't count anymore,
I love you the most,
I try to proximate you,
You are trembling,
You can't move.
The baker watches everything with
perseverance,
From behind the display,
Making a call to the disaster services.
I jog away.
This event could have been different,
But things always remain the same.
Some fairies can never be
Attained.

I LEAVE YOUR HAND

Vines and creepers,
Smoking reefers,
Drinking Jack Daniel's
On that cliff,
Which had the view,
Of a valley beneath,
As a drone spots you,
Silently observes you,
As you finish
Your fish and chips.
A dog within your confine
Sniffs,
You are at the edge,
Sitting all alone,
Engrossed in your thoughts,
As you just had a breakup,
With that heartless man,
At the pier.
He loves another,
But needed you as an accessory,
A 'fuck-buddy'.
You let these thoughts,
Consume you too much,
As you feel the urge,
To jump.

And you kiss,
Your German shepherd,
On its lips.
He makes sounds,
That are out of this realm,
Knowing what you would do next,
As you step away,
From the smooch,
You shift more,
Towards the edge;
You jump off.
You are in a slant,
But you feel a force,
A hand pulls you back.
It was me.
I had gone hunting,
With my drone,
I usually spot,
Animals.
But I could only see you,
For a long time;
Your features,
Your eyes,
Your hair,
Your half-smile,
Since you were miserable.
You don't even know me,
I am your neighbour.
I heard the fights,

On phone you would pour out,
Your passion to someone,
Who didn't care much,
About your well being,
As such
I cared.
But I was inconspicuous,
You always treaded through me,
I was shy and apprehensive.
But now,
That you wanted to destroy your life,
I had to make a movement,
I had to preclude you,
From yourself.
I don't expect you to be mine,
But I expect you,
Not to be his too.
With those feelings,
I plant a kiss,
On your
Hand,
As I toss you right back,
Into the
Abyss.
Now, nobody
Can attain you.

STRANGER

Oh! Stranger beloved,
You and I,
Rocked our universe,
Just for one night.
I didn't even catch your name.
Oh! How I miss you.
We were a thousand miles away,
From reality and,
Imbibed into,
Space and time.
It didn't matter,
How we met.
Whatever we had,
Was intense.
Now every breath
I take,
Has a tinge of you;
Every lovemaking,
With another,
Reminds me of you.
Getting up,
Getting down,
Getting ready for work,
Driving around,
I think of you,

As if,
A part of your soul,
Is left in me.
I touch myself sometimes,
Remembering your face.
Now that memory turns blurry.
Where are you now?
What must you be doing?
Are you even alive?
Or are we both deceased and away,
From constant reality?
Should we be together,
Or should we remain
Separated
Forever?
Is life
A psychedelic experience?

THE CANNIBAL

She sat there,
A Trans woman,
Looking at
The couple beneath.
They fought,
Like no tomorrow.
They fought,
Almost annihilating each other,
Over a small dispute,
Of how the boy talked,
With her mother,
At a family dinner.
He wanted to kill her,
But the cannibal up,
Smelt blood.
As the fight exceeded
Expectations,
The girl pulled out a dagger,
From her bra,
Swung it in the air,
Causing a laceration,
On his chest,
Through the white shirt he wore,
All bloody now.
The cannibal jumped down from above,

The girl ran with all her might,
The man quivered,
And then made a U-turn,
Towards,
Love's never-ending paradise,
Away from the cannibal,
With vampire's teeth.
He tried to run,
But the cannibal ran
After him,
Without much effort.
She reached for his shirt,
Caught him in his tracks,
In front.
The blood made her go crazy,
The man was already in shock.
She took him,
To the building that stood
Besides them.
She then smashed the man's head,
With a rock,
And blood spattered,
All over the white wall.
She drags the now dead body,
To the alleyway,
But then hears
Two gunshots,
Then looks at
Who shot them—

It was the girlfriend,
Who had gone back,
To the car,
Got the gun,
From a hush-hush compartment.
But the cannibal,
Aimed right at her,
Started running towards her,
As she almost reached the neck,
Of the stunned figure,
The trans cannibal
Falls.

THE REAL MEANING OF WINTER

When winter arrived,
You curled up
Into your comfortable sofa,
With a cup of hot chocolate,
Dripping on the sides,
Due to the marshmallow that
You forced into it.
I was beside you,
I licked the sides.
Hot chocolate should never be wasted;
But am I on the side?
You see,
I have been on vacation,
I told you.
But, I was living
In the basement,
In that spare room,
Which you never came to.
I said I'm going to Sydney,
For a week.
I had full faith in you,
That you would never cheat.
But I have heard the thumping and thuds,
From our living room,

From this couch we sit on,
And the floor.
The clamours penetrate through,
To the basement below,
I heard each moan,
I heard each tête-à-tête,
Where it was even discussed,
Of letting me go.
But I wonder,
Am I the side-bitch,
Or she, whom you made love to,
In my absence?
Or are we both,
Meaningless
To you?

ROMANTIC MONSOON

The monsoon,
That love we have,
Mislaid,
Those emotions that once were,
So pure,
Now drenched,
In the rain,
Just like us that day,
Together at a fort,
As the rain came unannounced,
Made us wet.
I liked your hair,
Wet;
The texture changed!
We canoodled,
As the downpour got the best of us,
Camouflaged us from the sight,
Of other onlookers,
In their fortress shelters.
But we
Started making love,
On the fort-top,
As the gorge beneath,
Observed us,
Getting lost into temptation.

Then as we emanated together,
You got up,
Feeling guilty of what we did.
For no apparent reason,
You get a panic attack,
Your period hasn't come yet,
From the last intimate session,
And you stealthily move around,
With your slipper in waning grip,
Due to over usage,
Causes you
To slip and
Fall,
Into the valley of
Demise.

I CAN'T SLEEP ANYMORE

From the stem arises
Thorns,
A modified branch or stem it is.
From it,
The most beautiful flowers bloom,
To remain untouched,
Only to find morning dew,
All over,
On a misty morning,
As we lay
On our bed,
Just like yesterday,
Today is a new day,
To begin with,
You,
To search for our love,
That was now a distant hallucination.
But,
I always remained a handsome petal with
A Reddish hue,
Until you,
Plucked me out,
Of my bunch.
But you!

You don't know how to,
Preserve me,
You made me grow,
Stale.
I lost my pigment,
I lost my Lustre,
No dewdrops cover me,
Anymore.
I can see now,
A blackish moss,
Grow all over me;
I'll be in fragments soon.
But you,
You sleep with no trouble,
On our bed,
Besides me,
Unruffled.
But me!
I can't sleep,
I am going to wither down,
Soon!

BIGGEST FUCKING REGRET

At the cafe,
I see the barista,
Tend to you.
You had a
Golden hair-clip,
Which could fall,
Anytime soon.
I was behind you,
I witness you,
As you turned around after ordering
Your americano with
A side of almond milk;
A peculiar order.
You mix your milk
From the side?
Then you see me,
And your expression,
From the coquettish happy one,
Turns to an eclipse
On your face,
As you recognise me—
The one you slaughtered,
In the parking,
Just because I saw you,

With another man,
At the club.
You loaded me into your boot space,
You dumped me into the ghat,
My body remained there for a while.
In panic you forgot to check my pulse rate,
I was taken care of by a local old lady,
Who came to pluck oranges from the orchard,
Near where my body lay;
She saved me and resuscitated me.
I have recovered now,
Lost my poise for a while,
Couldn't stride,
But now I can.
I ask you to sit with me,
And force you to deliberate,
About why you did,
What you did.
I might apprise,
The law-enforcement,
But I love you even now,
And that is my
Biggest fucking regret.

I HIT ON YOU

I see you on Instagram,
You do reels,
For sexual-freedom;
What does that even mean?
You want people,
To explore their
Sexuality?
But your boldness to do so,
In public,
Really is something,
Being a girl,
In this society where,
Even sexual education,
Is a sin sometimes.
You are here,
Doing the complete opposite.
In extreme.
As I see you in that show of yours,
In that hotel,
I come up to you,
You recognise me
From our private conversations,
On Instagram.
You say you would meet me,
To come up backstage later.

As I do just that,
You take me in your embrace,
And you tell me
In a whisper,
"Help me! My videos
Are viral
On the dark web,
And there is someone here
Who is going to kill me!"
I say,
"Don't panic
Nothing of that sort
Will happen."
As you
Keep calm and,
Take me to your room,
As we start with a kiss,
I surprise you with a bottle,
Of your favourite wine,
Freshly plucked,
From your favourite
Vineyard.
As I watch you
Drink a sip,
And get paralysed,
As you keep staring at me,
Like Julius Caesar
Staring at Brutus,
The only difference is,

Your mouth is paralysed,
You can't say,
YOU TOO, BRUTUS!
I am a hitman
By occupation you see,
The occult is where
I survive;
I got an order to kill you,
From the dark web.
You were right.
My client will be so delighted,
Proud of me,
A trip to the Bahamas,
Is where you will see me,
Partying.

SHE LIKES GIRLS

At the butcher shop
We both go,
The butcher
Drives into meat,
His knife
Now crimson,
As pieces of muscle
Fall down,
Into a reservoir,
And all the juices flow
Down into a tunnel.
Strawberry-red coloured.
You puke at the sight,
A good-hearted being,
You always wanted to be vegan;
But I wanted my
Protein,
Paneer doesn't do much to me you see.
As the butcher hands over
Cut pieces of
Tender meat,
I take care of you,
And take you out,
Before you retch more.
But this meat-fiasco is nothing,

Compared to you,
Being an infidel,
In that hotel where,
I seized you with a girl.
You were a lesbian,
I didn't mind that.
But why did you
Marry me?
Why did you
Wreck my life?
All I wanted,
Was to be with you,
And be a good husband,
Fulfil your needs,
But I was forlorn,
When I saw such an
Eventful sight.
I go out to the butcher shop
That night,
I buy the whole stock,
Alive.
I set the chicken free,
I wanted to daze you,
I wanted to demonstrate to you,
That lives can be saved.
Now I'm left with,
A flock of chickens,
In my backyard,
Saved.

But I deliver them back,
To the butcher,
Today.
I didn't want to surprise you,
Anymore.
I would rather save my own life,
Today.
I don't return home,
I go to my favourite place,
To my ex,
Is where I belong.
I have lost touch with actuality.
Anyways,
With all of these
Disastrous outcomes,
Of my life,
Who would have thought,
I would marry
A lesbian?

THE DISTANT LOVER

I see you on the bench,
You clutch your hand,
Covering your face,
I see streams of salty water,
Drip out through the
Lateral angle of your eyes,
On your cheeks they puddle up,
Before they fall.
You looked vibrant and striking,
Even when you were crying.
What made you cry?
When you were seventeen,
Your parents separated,
You and your mom,
Were left abandoned,
Torn hearts and
Worlds broken,
To infinite fragments.
In denial you lived,
That nothing bad could
Ever happen.
But now you believe,
In the darkness,
That showed up,
In your life,

Unannounced.
As I gape at you,
Wanting to care,
I approach you,
But you push me away.
You are unapproachable now,
I'm a mess though,
I couldn't pick myself up,
I tried to make you blissful.
But your swollen red eyes,
Were so much in transgression,
In chaos you survived.
But what about me,
Your distant lover,
Who has observed everything,
But has no role to play,
To make things
Right?

THE DARK BUTTERFLY

There is something beneath your skin,
It crawls like
Those pictures of bugs,
On Google,
But darker,
With faces that look like
Metamorphosis
Has stuck
In between,
So disfigured,
So intricately outward—
I am spellbound by you.
But I see you have,
Something
Crawling under your skin,
Let me take a blade,
And cut it out.
For only I should be
Skulking,
Under your skin,
Not some ancient,
Creepy-crawly,
That will evolve and then,
Go away,
For eternity,

Leaving you stranded,
And solo.
But just be advised,
Once you are sure,
I will never bequeath you,
I will
Leave you
Too.

BUTTER CHICKEN

At the Dhaba
I take you,
I am broke you see,
We order butter chicken,
The oil forms a thick layer
On top,
I dip into it
My Naan
Dipped in oil,
Dipped into
The buttery chicken,
And I take my hand,
To feed myself,
Not you.
I am not that romantic.
But as the scotch hits me,
I lose my inhibition,
And ask you,
To feed me,
Butter chicken.
But instead,
You come beside me,
And start to
French-kiss me,
At the Dhaba!

As everyone looks,
I feel shy and amused.
But then,
You feed me,
With your hands melting away,
With the butter chicken.
But then I need to smoke,
I smoke a puff,
On your face.
You inhale it in.
You love,
The smell of Ash,
On your skin.
But I know,
You have smoked,
Cuban cigars,
With that other guy.
A gold digger you are.
I am still broke,
I need to break up,
With you.
But,
You see,
It's difficult,
To let a hottie like you,
Just get away,
With anything,
You want.
But then I see,

A Beamer parked,
In the parking.
A guy approaches us,
I recognise it's him,
I'm astonished,
As he removes a gun and,
Points it at me!
But you,
You told me you broke up with him.
"That's life!"
You say and
Just leave.
While I am left now,
With my bowl of
Unfinished butter chicken.
It tasted good though.
Dhaba food can't be
Wasted.
I finish it
All.

SWEATY DISDAIN

Beads of sweat,
On your forehead.
Beads of sweat,
On your back.
I can see it,
On the creases of your face.
I can see it on creases,
In other places.
I wipe the perspiration,
Off you.
But my secretions add
Up to yours,
Making us worse,
In the heat.
I tell you,
To put on the air conditioning.
I tell you.
But you are not listening,
So, I ruin the moment,
Get up from where we lay,
I put on the air conditioning.
It catches fire
Somehow.
You tell me you remember,
The electrician warned you,

About some wiring issue.
Damn it!
Now we have to run
Away,
As our wetness builds up,
More than what it was,
Just a moment
Back.

THE CHRONIC RAVER

The chronic raver,
Partying from the age of
Fifteen,
Techno,
Trance and
Psychedelic music,
Never getting tired,
A pure mystique,
Carrying in her purse,
Antacids, pee-cones and
Anti-emetics.
The chronic raver,
Always had it ready,
For everything.
The chronic raver,
Came in a trippy dress,
Where colours collided,
Where the orange shades,
And greens,
Melted,
Into the
Fellow raver's brains.
She caused everyone to be
Thrilled.
The chronic raver decided,

What to drink and when
It was enough,
The chronic raver,
Danced.
She asked, 'When is the party gonna end?
Fuck that!
Not now!'
The chronic raver took care of,
All the members.
Throughout the dark night,
She would come alive.
The chronic raver,
Found love,
In a non-raver,
Converted him,
Into a fucking rave-machine,
Lunatic,
She then,
Lost love,
Found love again,
With another fellow raver.
Whatever may happen,
The rave should never stop.
An assortment of,
Repeating DJs playing,
One of her special favourites,
A photograph to be taken,
After ten long years she awaited,
This fine moment.

The chronic raver,
Made everyone feel warm.
But who will keep
The chronic raver
Warm?
Who will take care
Of the being
Who takes care
Of all?

STRONGER

I need someone stronger
Than me,
Who can
Breathe in synchronisation,
With me,
Together.
Match my strength,
And surpass it.
I see you,
Coming close to me,
At the bar.
You look
Stronger,
With your muscles,
Popping out.
But can you do me right?
Can you shake me,
Like lightning and thunder?
I take you to my place,
To another dimension.
You didn't ask me to,
But you followed me,
Like a canine,
Behind me,
Just after,

I, a girl, offered you a beer.
Isn't that the reverse happening?
As we close in together,
You uncork a bottle of wine,
While I am busy,
Uncorking you.
As we sail,
The seven seas together,
You aren't brutal enough,
You aren't that strong.
I toss you out,
Of my house,
I need something,
Stronger.
I wait for the one,
Who can make me,
Come
Stronger.

I LOVE IN THE DARK

The moonlight shines on me,
As I walk through my thoughts.
I see the past and present,
Collide,
As the darkness within consumes me,
As I melt into,
The fragments of my soul,
Picking up my pieces like a jigsaw,
Joining them together,
Only for them to be,
Disassembled again,
Again, and again,
In infinite ways,
As I try,
To figure life out,
And see the truth,
Beneath the lies that layer them.
I cannot distinguish,
Myself in the mirror.
I see an organism,
Appear in front of me;
It has no face.
But I observe it,
Excavating deep into me,
Deeper than a waterfall.

I resonate,
Deeper than life itself.
I try to love myself,
But success never finds its way,
To me.
I dig deeper,
Till I lose track of time,
Till I
Lose myself in
Time,
Till I Grey myself
Out
Of this cage called life.
The only meaning,
I find is
To Love,
In The
Dark,
And to
Decay.

ABOUT THE AUTHOR

Dr. Pratik Bhat, MD, is not only a distinguished pathologist but also a captivating poet whose words delve into the shadows of the human soul. Amidst the rigors of medical practice, Dr. Bhat finds solace in crafting dark poetry that explores the intricacies of love, loss, and the enigmatic depths of emotion. With a keen eye for detail honed through years of medical study and practice, his poetry resonates with a haunting beauty that mirrors the complexities of the human condition. Each verse is a testament to their mastery of language and their ability to navigate the delicate balance between light and darkness. His published works include: *Will You Cheat on Me, Baby?*, *Do I Get to Make You Mine?*, the *Darker Than Black series*, and *You Shattered My Soul!*. Dr. Bhat is dedicated to walking over 10 kilometers daily and indulges in an excessive amount of black coffee. When he's not penning his next bestseller, you'll find him immersed in books, coffee in hand, and miles underfoot.

www.ingramcontent.com/pod-product-compliance
Lightning Source LLC
Chambersburg PA
CBHW071340140726
47996CB00005B/2059